Collected Poetry

A. B. Paterson

ESPRIOS.COM
ESPRIOS DIGITAL PUBLISHING

Collected Poetry

By

Andrew Barton Paterson

CONTENTS

El Mahdi to the Australian Troops
The Bushfire
The Deficit Demon
Our Mat
Uncle Bill
The Sausage Candidate
Who is Kater Anyhow?
The Hypnotist
The Maori Pig Market
The Ballad of G. R. Dibbs
The Duties of an Aide-de-Camp
Behind the Scenes
Reconstruction
Tom Collins
The Ghost of the Murderer's Hut
A Triolet
The Wreck of the Golfer
The Sydney Cup
The Federal Bus Conductor and the Old Lady
A Rule of the A.J.C.
The Lost Leichhardt
Investigating Flora
Commandeering
The Rum Parade
Now Listen to Me and I'll Tell You My Views
The Ballad of Cockatoo Dock
The Ballad of that P.N.
Policeman G.
Gone Down
The Ballad of the Carpet Bag
A Nervous Governor-General
The Fitzroy Blacksmith
The Seven Ages of Wise
The Rhyme of the O'Sullivan
Ave Caesar
The Premier and the Socialist
The Ballad of M. T. Nutt and His Dog
The Man from Goondiwindi, Q.
The Dam that Keele Built
The Incantation
A Motor Courtship

Maxims of Hafiz
The Dauntless Three
Old Schooldays
We're All Australians Now
Australia Today 1916
The Army Mules
Swinging the Lead
Moving On
Hawker, the Standard Bearer
Cassidy's Epitaph
Boots
The Old Tin Hat
The Quest Eternal
That Half-Crown Sweep

Collected Poetry

EL MAHDI TO THE AUSTRALIAN TROOPS

And wherefore have they come, this warlike band,
That o'er the ocean many a weary day
That o'er the ocean many a weary day
Have tossed; and now beside Suakim's Bay,
With faces stern and resolute, do stand,
Waking the desert's echoes with the drum—
Men of Australia, wherefore have ye come?

To keep the Puppet Khedive on the throne,
To strike a blow for tyranny and wrong,
To crush the weak and aid the oppressing strong!
Regardless of the hapless Fellah's moan,
Regardless of the hapless Fellah's moan,
To force the payment of the Hebrew loan,
Squeezing the tax like blood from out the stone?

And fair Australia, freest of the free,
Is up in arms against the freeman's fight;
And with her mother joined to crush the right—
Has left her threatened treasures o'er the sea,
Has left her land of liberty and law
To flesh her maiden sword in this unholy war.

Enough! God never blessed such enterprise—
England's degenerate Generals yet shall rue
Brave Gordon sacrificed, when soon they view
The children of a thousand deserts rise
To drive them forth like sand before the gale—
God and the Prophet! Freedom will prevail.

The Bulletin, 28 February 1885

THE BUSHFIRE
An Allegory

'Twas on the famous Empire run,
  Whose sun does never set,
Whose grass and water, so they say,
  Have never failed them yet —
They carry many million sheep,
  Through seasons dry and wet.

They call the homestead Albion House,
  And then, along with that,
There's Welshman's Gully, Scotchman's Hill,
  And Paddymelon Flat:
And all these places are renowned
  For making jumbucks fat.

And the out-paddocks — holy frost!
  There wouldn't be no sense
For me to try and tell you half
  They really are immense;
A man might ride for days and weeks
  And never strike a fence.

But still for years they never had
  Been known a sheep to lose;
Old Billy Gladstone managed it,
  And you can bet your shoes
He'd scores of supers under him,
  And droves of jackaroos.

Old Billy had an eagle eye,
  And kept his wits about —
If any chaps got trespassing
  He quickly cleared 'em out;
And coves that used to "work a cross",
  They hated him, no doubt.

But still he managed it in style,
  Until the times got dry,
And Billy gave the supers word
  To see and mind their eye —

"If any paddocks gets a-fire
I'll know the reason why."

Now on this point old Bill was sure,
  Because, for many a year,
Whenever times got dry at all,
  As sure as you are here,
The Paddymelon Flat got burnt,
  Which Bill thought rather queer.

He sent his smartest supers there
  To try and keep things right.
No use! The grass was always dry—
  They'd go to sleep at night,
And when they woke they'd go and find
  The whole concern alight.

One morning it was very hot—
  The sun rose in a haze;
Old Bill was cutting down some trees
  (One of his little ways);
A black boy came hot-foot to say
  The Flat was in a blaze.

Old Bill he swears a fearful oath
  And lets the tommy fall
Says he: "I'll take this business up,
  And fix it once for all;
If this goes on the cursed run
  Will send us to the wall."

So he withdrew his trespass suits,
  He'd one with Dutchy's boss—
In prosecutions criminal
  He entered nolle pros.,
But these were neither here nor there—
  They always meant a loss.

And off to Paddymelon Flat
  He started double-quick
Drayloads of men with lots of grog
  Lest heat should make them sick,
And all the strangers came around

To see him do the trick.

And there the fire was flaming bright,
 For miles and miles it spread,
And many a sheep and horse and cow
 Were numbered with the dead —
The super came to meet Old Bill,
 And this is what he said:

"No use, to try to beat it out,
 'Twill dry you up like toast,
I've done as much as man can do,
 Although I never boast;
I think you'd better chuck it up,
 And let the jumbucks roast."

Then Bill said just two words:
 "You're sacked,"
And pitches off his coat,
 And pitches off his coat,
And wrenches down a blue gum bough
 And clears his manly throat,

And into it like threshing wheat
 Right sturdily he smote.
And beat the blazing grass until
 His shirt was dripping wet;
And all the people watched him there
 To see what luck he'd get,

"Gosh! don't he make the cinders fly,"
 And, "Golly, don't he sweat!"
But though they worked like Trojans all,
 The fire still went ahead
So far as you could see around,
 The very skies were red,

Sometimes the flames would start afresh,
 Just where they thought it dead.
His men, too, quarrelled 'mongst themselves
 And some coves gave it best
And some said, "Light a fire in front,
 And burn from east to west"

But Bill, he still kept sloggin' in,
  And never took no rest.
Then, through the crowd a cornstalk kid
  Come ridin' to the spot
Says he to Bill, "Now take a spell,
  You're lookin' very 'ot,

And if you'll only listen, why,
  I'll tell you what is what.
"These coves as set your grass on fire,
  There ain't no mortal doubt,
I've seen 'em ridin' here and there,
  And pokin' round about;

It ain't no use your workin' here,
  Until you finds them out.
"See yonder, where you beat the fire —
  It's blazin' up again,
And fires are starting right and left
  On Tipperary plain,

Beating them out is useless quite,
  Unless Heaven sends the rain."
Then Bill, he turns upon the boy,
  "Oh, hold your tongue, you pup!"
But a cinder blew across the creek
  While Bill stopped for a sup,
And fired the Albion paddocks, too —
  It was a bitter cup;
Old Bill's great heart was broke at last,
  He had to chuck it up.

Moral

The run is England's Empire great,
  The fire is the distress
That burns the stock they represent —
  Prosperity you'll guess.
And the blue gum bough is the Home Rule Bill
  That's making such a mess.

And Ireland green, of course I mean
  By Paddymelon Flat;

All men can see the fire, of course,
 Spreads on at such a bat,
But who are setting it alight,
 I cannot tell you that.

But this I think all men will see,
 And hold it very true
"Don't quarrel with effects until
 The cause is brought to view."
What is the cause? That cornstalk boy
 He seemed to think he knew.

The Bulletin, 12 June 1886

THE DEFICIT DEMON
A Political Ballad

It was the lunatic poet escaped from the local asylum,
Loudly he twanged on his banjo and sang with his voice like a saw-mill,
While as with fervour he sang there was borne o'er the shuddering wildwood,
Borne on the breath of the poet a flavour of rum and of onions.

He sang of the Deficit Demon that dwelt in the Treasury Mountains,
How it was small in its youth and a champion was sent to destroy it:
Dibbs he was called, and he boasted, "Soon will I wipe out the Monster,"
But while he was boasting and bragging the monster grew larger and larger.

One day as Dibbs bragged of his prowess in daylight the Deficit met him,
Settled his hash in one act and made him to all men a byword,
Sent him, a raving ex-Premier, to dwell in the shades of oblivion,
And the people put forward a champion known as Sir Patrick the Portly.

As in the midnight the tom-cat who seeketh his love on the house top,
Lifteth his voice up in song and is struck by the fast whizzing brickbat,
Drops to the ground in a swoon and glides to the silent hereafter,
So fell Sir Patrick the Portly at the stroke of the Deficit Demon.

Then were the people amazed and they called for the champion of champions
Known as Sir 'Enry the Fishfag unequalled in vilification.
He is the man, said the people, to wipe out the Deficit Monster,
If nothing else fetches him through he can at the least talk its head off.

So he sharpened his lance of Freetrade and he practised in loud-mouthed abusing,
"Poodlehead," "Craven," and "Mole-eyes" were things that he purposed to call it,
He went to the fight full of valour and all men are waiting the issue,
Though they know not his armour nor weapons excepting his power of abusing.

Loud sang the lunatic poet his song of the champions of valour
Until he was sighted and captured by fleet-footed keepers pursuing,
To whom he remarked with a smile as they ran him off back to the madhouse,
"If you want to back Parkes I'm your man—here's a cool three to one on the Deficit."

The Bulletin, 5 March 1887

OUR MAT

It came from the prison this morning,
 Close-twisted, neat-lettered, and flat;
It lies the hall doorway adorning,
 A very good style of a mat.

Prison-made! how the spirit is moven
 As we think of its story of dread
What wiles of the wicked are woven
 And spun in its intricate thread!

The letters are new, neat and nobby,
 Suggesting a masterly hand
Was it Sikes, who half-murdered the bobby,
 That put the neat D on the "and"?

Some banker found guilty of laches —
 It's always called laches, you know —
Had Holt any hand in those Hs?
 Did Bertrand illumine that 0?

That T has a look of the gallows,
 That A's a triangle, I guess;
Was it one of the Mount Rennie fellows
 Who twisted the strands of the S?

Was it made by some "highly connected",
 Who is doing his spell "on his head",
Or some wretched woman detected
 In stealing her children some bread?

Does it speak of a bitter repentance
 For the crime that so easily came?
Of the wearisome length of the sentence,
 Of the sin, and the sorrow, and shame?

A mat! I should call it a sermon
 On sin, to all sinners addressed;
It would take a keen judge to determine
 Whether writer or reader is best.

Though the doorway be hard as a pavestone,
 I rather would use it than that—
I'd as soon wipe my boots on a gravestone,
 As I would on that Darlinghurst mat!

The Bulletin, 2 April 1887

UNCLE BILL
The Larrikin's Lament

My Uncle Bill! My Uncle Bill!
How doth my heart with anguish thrill!
For he, our chief, our Robin Hood,
Has gone to jail for stealing wood!
With tears and sobs my voice I raise
To celebrate my uncle's praise;
With all my strength, with all my skill,
I'll sing the song of Uncle Bill.

Convivial to the last degree,
An open-hearted sportsman he.
Did midnight howls our slumbers rob,
We said, "It's uncle 'on the job'."
When sounds of fight rang sharply out,
Then Bill was bound to be about,
The foremost figure in "the scrap",
A terror to the local "trap".

To drink, or fight, or maim, or kill,
Came all alike to Uncle Bill.
And when he faced the music's squeak
At Central Court before the beak,
How carefully we sought our fob
To pay his fine of forty bob!
Recall the happy days of yore
When Uncle Bill went forth to war!

When all the street with strife was filled
And both the traps got nearly killed.
When the lone cabman on the stand
Was "stoushed" by Bill's unaided hand,
And William mounted, filled with rum,
And drove the cab to kingdom come.
Remember, too, that famous fray
When the "Black-reds", who hold their sway

O'er Surry Hills and Shepherd's Bush,
Descended on the "Liver Push".
Who cheered both parties long and loud?

Who heaved blue metal at the crowd!
And sooled his bulldog, Fighting Bet,
To bite, haphazard, all she met?
And when the mob were lodged in gaol
Who telegraphed to me for bail?

And — here I think he showed his sense —
Who calmly turned Queen's evidence?
Enough! I now must end my song,
My needless anguish, why prolong?
From what I've said, you'll own, I'm sure,
That Uncle Bill was pretty "pure",
So, rowdies all, your glasses fill,
And — drink it standing — "Uncle Bill".

The Bulletin, 9 June 1888

THE SAUSAGE CANDIDATE
A Tale of the Elections

Our fathers, brave men were and strong,
 And whisky was their daily liquor;
They used to move the world along
 In better style than now — and quicker.
Elections then were sport, you bet!
 A trifle rough, there's no denying
When two opposing factions met
 The skin and hair were always flying.

When "cabbage-trees" could still be worn
 Without the question, "Who's your hatter?"
There dawned a bright election morn
 Upon the town of Parramatta.
A man called Jones was all the go
 The people's friend, the poor's protector;
A long, gaunt, six-foot slab of woe,
 He sought to charm the green elector.

Now, Jones had one time been trustee
 For his small niece, and he — the villain! —
Betrayed his trust most shamefully,
 And robbed the child of every shillin'.
He used to keep accounts, they say,
 To save himself in case of trouble;
Whatever cash he paid away
 He always used to charge it double.

He'd buy the child a cotton gown
 Too coarse and rough to dress a cat in,
And then he'd go and put it down
 And charge the price of silk or satin!
He gave her once a little treat,
 An outing down the harbour sunny,
And Lord! the bill for bread and meat,
 You'd think they all had eaten money!

But Jones exposed the course he took
 By carelessness — such men are ninnies.
He went and entered in his book

"Two pounds of sausages—two guineas."
Now this leaked out, and folk got riled,
 And said that Jones, "he didn't oughter".
But what cared Jones? he only smiled—
 Abuse ran off his back like water.

And so he faced the world content:
 His little niece—he never paid her:
And then he stood for Parliament,
 Of course he was a rank free trader.
His wealth was great, success appeared
To smile propitious on his banner,
 But Providence it interfered
In this most unexpected manner.

A person—call him Brown for short—
 Who knew the story of this stealer,
Went calmly down the town and bought
 Two pounds of sausage from a dealer,
And then he got a long bamboo
 And tied the sausage tightly to it;
Says he, "This is the thing to do,
 And I am just the man to do it.

"When Jones comes out to make his speech
 I won't a clapper be, nor hisser,
But with this long bamboo I'll reach
 And poke the sausage in his 'kisser'.
I'll bring the wretch to scorn and shame,
 Unless those darned police are nigh:
As sure as Brown's my glorious name,
 I'll knock that candidate kite-high."

The speech comes on—beneath the stand
 The people push and surge and eddy
But Brown waits calmly close at hand
 With all his apparatus ready;
And while the speaker loudly cries,
 "Of ages all, this is the boss age!"
Brown hits him square between the eyes,
 Exclaiming, "What's the price of sausage?"

He aimed the victuals in his face,
  As though he thought poor Jones a glutton.
And Jones was covered with disgrace
  Disgrace and shame, and beef and mutton.
His cause was lost—a hopeless wreck
  He crept off from the hooting throng;
Protection proudly ruled the deck,
  Here ends the sausage and the song.

The Bulletin, 9 February 1889

WHO IS KATER ANYHOW?

"Mr Henry Edward Kater, of Moss Vale, son-in-law of the late William Forster, has been appointed a member of the New South Wales Legislative Council." Daily paper

Why, oh why was Kater lifted
From the darkness, where he drifted
All unknown, and raised to honour,
Side by side with Dick O'Connor,
In the Council, free from row?
Who is Kater, anyhow?

Did he bid our armies rally,
Like the recent Billy Dalley?
Did he lend a Premier money,
Like—(No libels here, my sonny.—Ed. B.)
Was he, like John Davies, found
Very useful underground?

Not at all! his claim to 'glory
Rests on quite another story.
All obscure he rhight have tarried,
But he managed to get married—
And (to cut the matter shorter)
Married William Forster's daughter.

So when Henry Edward Kater
Goes to answer his Creator,
Will the angel at the wicket
Say, on reading Kater's ticket—
"Enter! for you're no impostor,
Son-in-law of Billy Forster!"

The Bulletin, 2 March 1889

THE HYPNOTIST

A man once read with a mind surprised
Of the way that people were "hypnotised";
By waving of hands you produced, forsooth,
A kind of trance where men told the truth!
His mind was filled with wond'ring doubt;
He grabbed his hat and he started out,
He walked the street and he made a "set"
At the first half-dozen folk he met.
He "tranced" them all, and without a joke
'Twas much as follows the subjects spoke:

First Man

"I am a doctor, London-made,
Listen to me and you'll hear displayed
A few of the tricks of the doctor's trade.
'Twill sometimes chance when a patient's ill
That a dose, or draught, or a lightning pill,
A little too strong or a little too hot,
Will work its way to a vital spot.
And then I watch with a sickly grin
While the patient 'passes his counters in'.
But when he has gone with his fleeting breath
I certify that the cause of death
Was something Latin, and something long,
And who is to say that the doctor's wrong!
So I go my way with a stately tread
While my patients sleep with the dreamless dead."

Next, Please

"I am a barrister, wigged and gowned;
Of stately presence and look profound.
Listen awhile till I show you round.
When courts are sitting and work is flush
I hurry about in a frantic rush.
I take your brief and I look to see
That the same is marked with a thumping fee;
But just as your case is drawing near
I bob serenely and disappear.

And away in another court I lurk
While a junior barrister does your work;
And I ask my fee with a courtly grace,
Although I never came near the case.
The loss means ruin to you, maybe,
But nevertheless I must have my fee!
For the lawyer laughs in his cruel sport
While his clients march to the Bankrupt Court."

Third Man

"I am a banker, wealthy and bold —
A solid man, and I keep my hold
Over a pile of the public's gold.
I am as skilled as skilled can be
In every matter of £ s. d.
I count the money, and night by night
I balance it up to a farthing right:
In sooth, 'twould a stranger's soul perplex
My double entry and double checks.
Yet it sometimes happens by some strange crook
That a ledger-keeper will 'take his hook'
With a couple of hundred thousand 'quid',
And no one can tell how the thing was did!"

Fourth Man

"I am an editor, bold and free.
Behind the great impersonal 'We'
I hold the power of the Mystic Three.
What scoundrel ever would dare to hint
That anything crooked appears in print!
Perhaps an actor is all the rage,
He struts his hour on the mimic stage,
With skill he interprets all the scenes —
And yet next morning I give him beans.
I slate his show from the floats to flies,
Because the beggar won't advertise.
And sometimes columns of print appear
About a mine, and it makes it clear
That the same is all that one's heart could wish —
A dozen ounces to every dish.
But the reason we print those statements fine

Is—the editor's uncle owns the mine."

The Last Straw

"A preacher I, and I take my stand
In pulpit decked with a gown and band
To point the way to a better land.
With sanctimonious and reverent look
I read it out of the sacred book
That he who would open the golden door
Must give his all to the starving poor.
But I vary the practice to some extent
By investing money at twelve per cent,
And after I've preached for a decent while
I clear for 'home' with a lordly pile.
I frighten my congregation well
With fear of torment and threats of hell,
Although I know that the scientists
Can't find that any such place exists.
And when they prove it beyond mistake
That the world took millions of years to make,
And never was built by the seventh day
And never was built by the seventh day
I say in a pained and insulted way
That 'Thomas also presumed to doubt',
And thus do I rub my opponents out.
For folks may widen their mental range,
But priest and parson, they never change."

With dragging footsteps and downcast head
The hypnotiser went home to bed,
And since that very successful test
He has given the magic art a rest;
Had he tried the ladies, and worked it right,
What curious tales might have come to light!

The Bulletin, 19 July 1890

THE MAORI PIG MARKET

In distant New Zealand, whose tresses of gold
 The billows are ceaselessly combing,
Away in a village all tranquil and old
I came on a market where porkers were sold—
 A market for pigs in the gloaming.

And Maoris in plenty in picturesque rig
 The lands of their forefathers roaming,
Were weighing their swine, whether little or big,
For purchasers paid by the weight of the pig
 The weight of the pig in the gloaming.

And one mighty chieftain, I grieve to relate,
 The while that his porker was foaming
And squealing like fifty—that Maori sedate,
He leant on the pig just to add to its weight
 He leant on the pig in the gloaming.

Alas! For the buyer, an Irishman stout
 O'Grady, I think, his cognomen—
Perceived all his doings, and, giving a shout,
With the butt of his whip laid him carefully out
 By the side of his pig in the gloaming.

A terrible scrimmage did straightway begin,
 And I thought it was time to be homing,
For Maoris and Irish were fighting like sin
'Midst war-cries of "Pakeha!" "Batherashin!"
 As I fled from the spot in the gloaming.

The Bulletin, 22 November 1890

THE BALLAD OF G. R. DIBBS

This is the story of G.R.D.,
Who went on a mission across the sea
To borrow some money for you and me.

This G. R. Dibbs was a stalwart man
Who was built on a most extensive plan,
And a regular staunch Republican.

But he fell in the hands of the Tory crew
Who said, "It's a shame that a man like you
Should teach Australia this nasty view.

"From her mother's side she should ne'er be gone,
And she ought to be glad to be smiled upon,
And proud to be known as our hanger-on."

And G. R. Dibbs, he went off his peg
At the swells who came for his smiles to beg
And the Prince of Wales—who was pulling his leg

And he told them all when the wine had flown,
"The Australian has got no land of his own,
His home is England, and there alone."

So he strutted along with the titled band
And he sold the pride of his native land
For a bow and a smile and a shake of the hand.

And the Tory drummers they sit and call:
"Send over your leaders great and small;
For the price is low, and we'll buy them all

"With a tinsel title, a tawdry star
Of a lower grade than our titles are,
And a puff at a Prince's big cigar."

And the Tories laugh till they crack their ribs
When they think how they purchased G. R. Dibbs.

The Bulletin, 27 August 1892

THE DUTIES OF AN AIDE-DE-CAMP

Oh, some folk think vice-royalty is festive and hilarious,
The duties of an A.D.C. are manifold and various,
So listen, whilst I tell in song,
The duties of an aide-de-tong.

 Whatsoever betide
 To the Governor's side
We must stick—or the public would eat him—
 For each bounder we see
 Says, "Just introduce me
To His Lordship—I'm anxious to meet him."

 Then they grab at his paw
 And they chatter and jaw
Till they'd talk him to death—if we'd let 'em—
 And the folk he has met,
 They are all in a fret,
Just for fear he might chance to forget 'em.

 When some local King Billy
 Is talking him silly,
Or the pound-keeper's wife has waylaid him,
 From folks of that stamp
 When he has to decamp
We're his aides to decamp—so we aid him.

 Then some feminine beauty
 Will come and salute ye,
She may be a Miss or a Madam,
 Or a man comes in view,
 Bails you up, "How de do!"
And you don't know the fellow from Adam!

 But you've got to keep sweet
 With each man that you meet,
And a trifle like this mustn't bar you,
 So you clutch at his fin,
 And you say, with a grin,
"Oh, delighted to see you—how are you?"

Then we do country shows
Where some prize-taker blows
Of his pig—a great, vast forty-stoner—
"See, my Lord! ain't he fine!
How is that for a swine!"
When it isn't a patch on its owner!

We fix up the dinners
For parsons and sinners
And lawyers and bishops and showmen,
And a judge of the court
We put next to a "sport",
And an Orangeman next to a Roman.

We send invitations
To all celebrations,
Some Nobody's presence entreating,
And the old folks of all
We invite to a ball,
And the young—to a grandmothers' meeting.

And when we go dancing,
Like cart-horses prancing,
We plunge where the people are thickenin';
And each gay local swell
Thinks it's "off" to dance well,
So he copies our style—ain't it sickenin'!

Then at banquets we dine
And swig cheap, nasty wine,
But the poor aide-de-camp mustn't funk it—
And they call it champagne,
But we're free to maintain,
That he feels real pain when he's drunk it.

Then our horses bestriding
We go out a-riding
Lest our health by confinement we'd injure;
You can notice the glare
Of the Governor's hair
When .the little boys say, "Go it, Ginger!"

Then some wandering lords—

They so often are frauds
This out-of-way country invading,
 If a man dresses well
 And behaves like a swell,
Then he's somebody's cook masquerading.

 But an out-and-out ass
 With a thirst for the glass
And the symptoms of drink on his "boko",
 Who is perpetually
 Pursuing the ballet,
He is always the "true Orinoco".

 We must slave with our quills—
 Keep the cash—pay the bills
Keep account of the liquor and victuals—
 So I think you'll agree
 That the gay A.D.C.
Has a life that's not all beer and skittles!

The Bulletin, 21 January 1893

BEHIND THE SCENES

The actor struts his little hour,
  Between the limelight and the band;
The public feel the actor's power,
  Yet nothing do they understand
Of all the touches here and there
  That make or mar the actor's part,
They never see, beneath the glare,
  The artist striving after art.

To them it seems a labour slight
  Where nought of study intervenes;
You see it in another light
  When once you've been behind the scenes.

For though the actor at his best
For though the actor at his best
  Is, like a poet, born not made,
He still must study with a zest
  And practise hard to learn his trade.
So, whether on the actor's form
  The stately robes of Hamlet sit,
Or as Macbeth he rave and storm,
  Or plays burlesque to please the pit,

'Tis each and all a work of art,
  That constant care and practice means —
The actor who creates a part
  Has done his work behind the scenes.

The Bulletin, 8 April 1893

RECONSTRUCTION
From a Farmer's Point of View

So, the bank has bust its boiler! And in six or seven year
  It will pay me all my money back—of course!
But the horse will perish waiting while the grass is germinating,
  And I reckon I'll be something like the horse.

There's the ploughing to be finished and the ploughmen want their pay,
  And I'd like to wire the fence and sink a tank;
But I own I'm fairly beat how I'm going to make ends meet
  With my money in a reconstructed bank.

"It's a safe and sure investment!" But it's one I can't afford,
  For I've got to meet my bills and pay the rent,
And the cash I had provided (so these meetings have decided)
  Shall be collared by the bank at three per cent.

I can draw out half my money, so they tell me, from the Crown;
  But—it's just enough to drive a fellow daft
My landlord's quite distressed, by this very bank he's pressed,
  And he'll sell me up, to pay his overdraft.

There's my nearest neighbour, Johnson, owed this self-same bank a debt,
  Every feather off his poor old back they pluck't,
For they set to work to shove him, and they sold his house above him,
  Lord! They never gave him time to reconstruct.

And their profits from the business have been twenty-five per cent,
  Which, I reckon, is a pretty tidy whack,
And I think it's only proper, now the thing has come a cropper,
  That they ought to pay a little of it back.

I have read about "reserve funds", "banking freeholds", and the like,
  Till I thought the bank had thousands of assets,
And it strikes me very funny that they take a fellow's money
  When they haven't got enough to pay their debts.

And they say they've lent my money, and they can't get paid it back.
  I know their rates per cent were tens and twelves;
And if now they've made a blunder after scooping all this plunder,
  Why, they ought to fork the money out themselves.

So all you bank shareholders, if you won't pay what you owe,
 You will find that on your bank will fall a blight;
And the reason is because it's simply certain that deposits
 Will be stopped, the bank will bust, and serve you right!

The Bulletin, 17 June 1893

TOM COLLINS

Who never drinks and never bets,
But loves his wife and pays his debts
And feels content with what he gets?
   Tom Collins.

Who has the utmost confidence
That all the banks now in suspense
Will meet their paper three years hence?
   Tom Collins.

Who reads the Herald leaders through,
And takes the Evening News for true,
And thought the Echo's jokes were new?
   Tom Collins.

Who is the patriot renowned
So very opportunely found
To fork up Dibbs's thousand pound?
   Tom Collins.

The Bulletin, 19 August 1893

THE GHOST OF THE MURDERER'S HUT

My horse had been lamed in the foot
 In the rocks at the back of the run,
So I camped at the Murderer's Hut,
 At the place where the murder was done.

The walls were all spattered with gore,
 A terrible symbol of guilt;
And the bloodstains were fresh on the floor
 Where the blood of the victim was spilt.

The wind hurried past with a shout,
 The thunderstorm doubled its din
As I shrank from the danger without,
 And recoiled from the horror within.

When lo! at the window a shape,
 A creature of infinite dread;
A thing with the face of an ape,
 And with eyes like the eyes of the dead.

With the horns of a fiend, and a skin
 That was hairy as satyr or elf,
And a long, pointed beard on its chin—
 My God! 'twas the Devil himself.

In anguish I sank on the floor,
 With terror my features were stiff,
Till the thing gave a kind of a roar,
 Ending up with a resonant "Biff!"

Then a cheer burst aloud from my throat,
 For the thing that my spirit did vex
Was naught but an elderly goat
 Just a goat of the masculine sex.

When his master was killed he had fled,
 And now, by the dingoes bereft,
The nannies were all of them dead,
 And only the billy was left.

So we had him brought in on a stage
 To the house where, in style, he can strut,
And he lives to a fragrant old age
 As the Ghost of the Murderer's Hut.

The Bulletin, 30 December 1893

A TRIOLET

Of all the sickly forms of verse,
 Commend me to the triolet.
It makes bad writers somewhat worse:
Of all the sickly forms of verse
That fall beneath a reader's curse,
 It is the feeblest jingle yet.
Of all the sickly forms of verse,
 Commend me to the triolet.

The Bulletin, 13 January 1894

THE WRECK OF THE GOLFER

It was the Bondi golfing man
 Drove off from the golf house tee,
And he had taken his little daughter
 To bear him company.

"Oh, Father, why do you swing the club
 And flourish it such a lot?"
"You watch it fly o'er the fences high!"
 And he tried with a brassey shot.

"Oh, Father, why did you hit the fence
 Just there where the brambles twine?"
And the father he answered never a word,
 But he got on the green in nine.

"Oh, Father, hark from behind those trees,
 What dismal yells arrive!"
"'Tis a man I ween on the second green,
 And I've landed him with my drive."

"Oh, Father, why does the poor Chinee
 Fall down on his knees and cry?"
"He taketh me for his Excellency,
 And he thinks once hit twice shy."

So on they fared to the waterhole,
 And he drove with a lot of dash,
But the balls full soon in the dread lagoon
 Fell down with a woeful splash.

"Oh, Father, why do you beat the sand
 Till it flies like the carded wool?"
And the father he answered never a word,
 For his heart was much too full.

"Oh, Father, why are they shouting 'fore'
 And screaming so lustily?"
But the father he answered never a word,
 A pallid corpse was he.

For a well-swung drive on the back of his head
  Had landed and laid him low.
Lord save us all from a fate like this
  When next to the links we go.

The Sydney Mail, 4 September 1897

SYDNEY CUP, 1899
An Outside Tip

Of course they all say if this Bobadil starts
  He'll settle 'em all in a flash:
For the pace he can go will be breaking their hearts,
  And he ends with the "Bobadil dash".
But there's one in the race is a fancy of mine
  Whenever the distance is far—
Crosslake! He's inbred to the Yattendon line,
  And we know what the Yattendons are.

His feet are his trouble: they're tender as gum!
  If only his feet are got straight,
If the field were all Bobadils—let 'em all come
  So long as they carry the weight.
For a three-year-old colt with nine-three on his back—
  Well, he needs to be rather a star!
And with seven stone ten we will trust the old black,
  For we know what the Yattendons are.

He is sired by Lochiel, which ensures that his pace
  Is enough, and a little to spare.
But the blood that will tell at the end of the race
  Is the blood of the Yattendon mare.
And this "Bobby" will find, when the whips are about,
  It's a very fast journey and far.
And there's just the least doubt—will he battle it out?
  But we know what the Yattendons are.

In the rest of the field there are some that can stay,
  And a few that can fly—while they last.
But the old black outsider will go all the way,
  And finish uncommonly fast.
If his feet last him out to the end of the trip—
  Bare-footed or shod with a bar
If he once gets this Bobadil under the whip,
  Then he'll show what the Yattendons are.

The Bulletin, 25 March 1899

THE FEDERAL BUS CONDUCTOR AND THE OLD LADY

Now 'urry, Mrs New South Wales, and come along of us,
We're all a-goin' ridin' in the Federation 'bus.
A fam'ly party, don't you know—yes, Queensland's comin', too.
You can't afford it! Go along! We've kep' box seat for you.
The very one of all the lot that can afford it best,
You'll only have to pay your share the same as all the rest.

You say your sons is workin' men, and can't afford to ride!
Well, all our sons is workin' men, a-smokin' up outside.
You think you might be drove to smash by some unskilful bloke!
Well, ain't we all got necks ourselves? And we don't want 'em broke.
You bet your life we're not such fools but what we'll do our best
To keep from harm—for harm to one is harm to all the rest.

Now, don't go trudgin' on alone, but get aboard the trap;
That basket, labelled "Capital",* you take it in your lap!
It's nearly time we made a start, so let's 'ave no more talk:
You 'urry up and get aboard, or else stop out and walk.
We've got a flag; we've got a band; our 'orses travels fast;
Ho! Right away, Bill! Let 'em go! The old 'un's come at last!**

The Bulletin, 17 June 1899

A RULE OF THE A.J.C.

Come all ye bold trainers attend to my song,
  It's a rule of the A.J.C.
You mustn't train ponies, for that's very wrong
  By the rules of the A.J.C.
You have to wear winkers when crossing the street,
For fear that a pony you'd happen to meet
If you hear one about, you must beat a retreat
  That's a rule of the A.J.C.

And all ye bold owners will find without fail
  By the rules of the A.J.C.,
The jockey boys' fees you must pay at the scale
  It's a rule of the A.J.C.
When your horse wins a fiver, you'll laugh, I'll be bound,
But you won't laugh so much by the time that you've found
That the fee to the boy is exactly ten pound!
  That's a rule of the A.J.C.

And all ye bold "Books" who are keeping a shop,
  In the rules of the A.J.C.,
There's a new regulation that says you must stop!
  That's a rule of the A.J.C.
You must give up your shop with its pipes and cigars
To an unlicensed man who is thanking his stars,
While you go and bet in the threepenny bars
  That's a rule of the A.J.C.

And all ye small jockeys who ride in a race,
  In the rules of the A.J.C.
If owners' instructions are "Don't get a place",
  By the rules of the A.J.C.,
You must ride the horse out—though, of course, if you do
You will get no more mounts, it's starvation to you.
But, bless you, you'll always find plenty to chew
  In the rules of the A.J.C.

The Bulletin, 26 August 1899

THE LOST LEICHHARDT

An English scientific society is fitting out a pioneering party to search for traces of the lost explorer Leichhardt

Another search for Leichhardt's tomb,
 Though fifty years have fled
Since Leichhardt vanished in the gloom,
 Our one Illustrious Dead!

But daring men from Britain's shore,
 The fearless bulldog breed,
Renew the fearful task once more,
 Determined to succeed.

Rash men, that know not what they seek,
 Will find their courage tried.
For things have changed on Cooper's Creek
 Since Ludwig Leichhardt died.

Along where Leichhardt journeyed slow
 And toiled and starved in vain;
These rash excursionists must go
 Per Queensland railway train.

Out on those deserts lone and drear
 The fierce Australian black
Will say—"You show it pint o' beer,
 It show you Leichhardt track!"

And loud from every squatter's door
 Each pioneering swell
Will hear the wild pianos roar
 The strains of "Daisy Bell".

The watchers in those forests vast
 Will see, at fall of night,
Commercial travellers bounding past
 And darting out of sight.

About their path a fearful fate
 Will hover always near.

A dreadful scourge that lies in wait—
The Longreach Horehound Beer!

And then, to crown this tale of guilt,
 They'll find some scurvy knave,
Regardless of their quest, has built
 A pub on Leichhardt's grave!

Ah, yes! Those British pioneers
 Had best at home abide,
For things have changed in fifty years
 Since Ludwig Leichhardt died.

The Bulletin, 14 October 1899

INVESTIGATING FLORA

'Twas in scientific circles
  That the great Professor Brown
Had a world-wide reputation
  As a writer of renown.
He had striven finer feelings
  In our natures to implant
By his Treatise on the Morals
  Of the Red-eyed Bulldog Ant.
He had hoisted an opponent
  Who had trodden unawares
On his "Reasons for Bare Patches
  On the Female Native Bears".
So they gave him an appointment
  As instructor to a band
Of the most attractive females
  To be gathered in the land.
'Twas a "Ladies' Science Circle" —
  Just the latest social fad
For the Nicest People only,
  And to make their rivals mad.
They were fond of "science rambles"
  To the country from the town —
A parade of female beauty
  In the leadership of Brown.
They would pick a place for luncheon
  And catch beetles on their rugs;
The Professor called 'em "optera"
  They called 'em "nasty bugs".
Well, the thing was bound to perish
  For no lovely woman can
Feel the slightest real interest
  In a club without a Man —
The Professor hardly counted
  He was crazy as a loon,
With a countenance suggestive
  Of an elderly baboon.
But the breath of Fate blew on it
  With a sharp and sudden blast,
And the "Ladies' Science Circle"
  Is a memory of the past.

There were two-and-twenty members,
 Mostly young and mostly fair,
Who had made a great excursion
 To a place called Dontknowwhere,
At the crossing of Lost River,
 On the road to No Man's Land.
There they met an old selector,
 With a stockwhip in his hand,
And the sight of so much beauty
 Sent him slightly "off his nut";
So he asked them, smiling blandly,
 "Would they come down to the hut?"
"I am come," said the Professor,
 In his thin and reedy voice,
"To investigate your flora,
 Which I hear is very choice."
The selector stared dumbfounded,
 Till at last he found his tongue:
"To investigate my Flora!
 Oh, you howlin' Brigham Young!
Why, you've two-and-twenty wimmen—
 Reg'lar slap-up wimmen, too!
And you're after little Flora!
 And a crawlin' thing like you!
Oh, you Mormonite gorilla!
 Well, I've heard it from the first
That you wizened little fellers
 Is a hundred times the worst!

But a dried-up ape like you are,
 To be marchin' through the land
With a pack of lovely wimmen
 Well, I cannot understand!"
"You mistake," said the Professor,
 In a most indignant tone
While the ladies shrieked and jabbered
 In a fashion of their own—
"You mistake about these ladies,
 I'm a lecturer of theirs;
I am Brown, who wrote the Treatise
 On the Female Native Bears!
When I said we wanted flora,
 What I meant was native flowers."

"Well, you said you wanted Flora,
 And I'll swear you don't get ours!
But here's Flora's self a-comin',
 And it's time for you to skip,
Or I'll write a treatise on you,
 And I'll write it with the whip!

Now, I want no explanations;
 Just you hook it out of sight,
Or you'll charm the poor girl some'ow!"
 The Professor looked in fright:
She was six feet high and freckled,
 And her hair was turkey-red.
The Professor gave a whimper,
 And threw down his bag and fled,
And the Ladies' Science Circle,
 With a simultaneous rush,
Travelled after its Professor,
 And went screaming through the bush!

At the crossing of Lost River,
 On the road to No Man's Land,
Where the grim and ghostly gumtrees
 Block the view on every hand,
There they weep and wail and wander,
 Always seeking for the track,
For the hapless old Professor
 Hasn't sense to guide 'em back;
And they clutch at one another,
 And they yell and scream in fright
As they see the gruesome creatures
 Of the grim Australian night;
And they hear the mopoke's hooting,
 And the dingo's howl so dread,
And the flying foxes' jabber
 From the gum trees overhead;
While the weird and wary wombats,
 In their subterranean caves,
Are a-digging, always digging,
 At those wretched people's graves;
And the pike-horned Queensland bullock,
 From his shelter in the scrub,
Has his eye on the proceedings

Collected Poetry

Of the Ladies' Science Club.

The Bulletin, 9 December 1899

COMMANDEERING

Our hero was a Tommy with a conscience free from care,
And such an open countenance that when he breathed the air
He mopped up all the atmosphere—so little went to spare
You could hardly say he breathed, he "commandeered" it.

For nowadays you'll notice when a man is "on the make",
And other people's property is anxious for to take,
We never use such words as "steal", or "collar", "pinch", or "shake".
No, the fashion is to say we "commandeered" it.

And our simple-minded hero used to grumble at his lot,
Said he, "This commandeerin's just a little bit too hot,
A fellow has to carry every blooming thing he's got;
Whatever he puts down they'll commandeer it."

So after much anxiety our simple-minded elf
He thought he'd do a little commandeering for himself,
And the first thing that he noticed was a bottle on a shelf
In a cottage, so he thought he'd commandeer it.

"What ho!" says he, "a bottle, and, by George, it's full of beer,
And no commanding officer to come and interfere.
Here's my own blooming health," says he, "I'm on the commandeer."
And without another word he commandeered it.

On his subsequent proceedings we must draw a little veil,
For the Boers had left some sheep dip in that bottle labelled "Ale";
But the doctor said he'd shift it—if all other methods fail,
We must use the stomach pump and commandeer it.

The Sydney Mail, 26 May 1900

THE RUM PARADE
Tune: "Ballyhooley"

Now ye gallant Sydney boys, who have left your household joys
 To march across the sea in search of glory,
I am very much afraid that you do not love parade,
 But the rum parade is quite another story.
For the influenza came and to spoil its little game,
 They ordered we should drink a curious mixture;
Though at first it frightened some, when they found it mostly rum,
 Parade became a very pleasant fixture.

Chorus

So it's forward the Brigade, if they'll hold a rum parade
 At Pretoria there's nothing to alarm ye;
And it's easy to be seen if they leave the quinine,
 Ye'll be there before the blessed British Army.

Then a corporal he come and he said I drank the rum,
 But the quinine never reached its destination;
For begob he up and swored that I threw it overboard,
 Sure my heart was filled with grief and indignation.

For I'm different to some, I prefer quinine to rum,
 And I only take the rum just as a favour,
And it's easy to be seen I'm so fond of the quinine,
 That I keep it lest the rum should spoil its flavour.

When we get to Africay we'll be landed straight away,
 And quartered with the troops of Queen Victoria;
And we hope they'll understand that the moment that we land
 We are ready for a march upon Pretoria.

And we'll pay off all the scores on old Kruger and his Boers,
 And just to prove our manners aren't a failure,
And to show we are not mean, shure we'll give them the quinine,
 And drink the rum in honour of Australia.

The Sydney Mail, 1900

NOW LISTEN TO ME AND I'LL TELL YOU MY VIEWS

Now listen to me and I'll tell you my views concerning the African war,
And the man who upholds any different views, the same is a rotten Pro-Boer!
(Though I'm getting a little bit doubtful myself, as it drags on week after week:
But it's better not ask any questions at all—let us silence all doubts with a shriek!)

And first let us shriek the unstinted abuse that the Tory Press prefer
De Wet is a madman, and Steyn is a liar, and Kruger a pitiful cur!
(Though I think if Oom Paul—as old as he is—were to walk down the Strand with his gun,
A lot of these heroes would hide in the sewers or take to their heels and run!
For Paul he has fought like a man in his day, but now that he's feeble and weak
And tired, and lonely, and old and grey, of course it's quite safe to shriek!)

And next let us join in the bloodthirsty shriek, Hooray for Lord Kitchener's "bag"!
For the fireman's torch and the hangman's cord—they are hung on the English Flag!
In the front of our brave old army! Whoop! the farmhouse blazes bright.
And their women weep and their children die—how dare they presume to fight!

For none of them dress in a uniform, the same as by rights they ought.
They're fighting in rags and in naked feet, like Wallace's Scotchmen fought!
(And they clothe themselves from our captured troops—and they're catching them every week;
And they don't hang them—and the shame is ours, but we cover the shame with a shriek!)

And, lastly, we'll shriek the political shriek as we sit in the dark and doubt;
Where the Birmingham Judas* led us in, and there's no one to lead us out.
And Rosebery**—whom we depended upon! Would only the Oracle speak!
"You go to the Grocers," says he, "for your laws!" By heavens! it's time to shriek!

The Bulletin, 29 March 1902

THE BALLAD OF COCKATOO DOCK

Of all the docks upon the blue
There was no dockyard, old or new,
To touch the dock at Cockatoo.

Of all the ministerial clan
There was no nicer, worthier man
Than Admiral O'Sullivan.

Of course we mean E. W.
O'Sullivan, the hero who
Controlled the dock at Cockatoo.

To workmen he explained his views—
"You need not toil unless you choose,
Your only work is drawing screws."

And sometimes to their great surprise
When votes of censure filled the skies
He used to give them all a rise.

"What odds about a pound or two?"
Exclaimed the great E. W.
O'Sullivan at Cockatoo.

The dockyard superintendent, he
Was not at all what he should be—
He sneered at all this sympathy.

So when he gave a man the sack
O'Sullivan got on his track
And straightway went and fetched him back.

And with a sympathetic tear
He'd say, "How dare you interfere,
You most misguided engineer?

"Your sordid manners please amend—
No man can possibly offend
Who has a Member for a friend.

"With euchre, or a friendly rub,
And whisky from the nearest 'pub',
We'll make the dockyard like a club.

"Heave ho, my hearties, play away,
We'll do no weary work today.
What odds—the public has to pay!

"And if the public should complain
I'll go to Broken Hill by train
To watch McCarthy making rain."

And there, with nothing else to do
No doubt the great E. W.
Will straightway raise McCarthy's screw.

The Evening News, 9 July 1903

THE BALLAD OF THAT P.N.

The shades of night had fallen at last,
When through the house a shadow passed,
That once had been the Genial Dan,
But now become a desperate man,
At question time he waited near,
And on the Premier's startled ear
A voice fell like half a brick
"Did ye, or did ye not, pay Crick
    Did ye?"

By land and sea the Premier sped,
But found his foe where'er he fled,
The sailors swore—with whitened lip—
That Neptune swam behind the ship:
When to the stern the Premier ran,
Behold, 'twas no one else but Dan,
And through the roaring of the gale
That clarion voice took up the tale,
"Ahoy there! Answer, straight and slick!
Did not the Ministry pay Crick
    Did they?"

In railway trains he sought retreat,
But soon, from underneath the seat,
With blazing eye and bristling beard,
His ancient enemy appeared,
And like a boiling torrent ran
The accents of the angry Dan—
"Tell me, John See, and tell me quick
Did not ye pay your shares to Crick
    Did ye?"

The Evening News, 15 July 1903

POLICEMAN G.
Air: "Widow McGrath"

To Policeman G. the Inspector said:
"When you pass the 'shops' you must turn your head;
If you took a wager, that would be a sin;
So you'll earn no stripes if you run them in."
 Mush-a-ring-tiy-ah,
 Fol-de-diddle-doh!

To the House Committee, the Inspector said:
"'Tis a terrible thing how the gamblers spread,
For they bet on the Steeple, and they bet on the Cup,
And the magistrates won't lock them up."
 Mush-a-ring-tiy-ah,
 Fol-de-diddle-doh!

But Policeman G., as he walks his beat,
Where the gamblers are—up and down the street—
Says he: "What's the use to be talkin' rot
If they'd make me a sergeant, I could cop the lot!"
 With my ring-tiy-ah,
 Fol-de-diddle-doh!

"But, bedad if you start to suppress the 'shop',
Then the divil only knows where you're going to stop;
For the rich and the poor, they would raise a din,
If at Randwick I ran fifty thousand in."
 Mush-a-ring-tiy-ah,
 Fol-de-diddle-doh!

"Though ye must not box—nor shpit—nor bet,
I'll find my way out to Randwick yet;
For I'm shtandin' a pound—and it's no disgrace
On Paddy Nolan's horse—for the Steeplechase!"
 Mush-a-ring-tiy-ah,
 Fol-de-diddle-doh!

The Evening News, 9 September 1903

GONE DOWN

To the voters of Glen Innes 'twas O'Sullivan that went,
  To secure the country vote for Mister Hay.
So he told 'em what he'd borrowed, and he told 'em what he'd spent,
  Though extravagance had blown it all away.
Said he, "Vote for Hay, my hearties, and wherever we may roam
  We will borrow, undismayed by Fortune's frown!"
When he got his little banjo, and he sang them "Home, Sweet Home!"
  Why, it made a blessed horse fall down.

Then he summoned his supporters, and went spouting through the bush,
  To assure them that he'd build them roads galore,
If he could but borrow something from the "Plutocratic Push",
  Though he knew they wouldn't lend him any more.
With his Coolangatta Croesus, who was posing for the day
  As a Friend of Labour, just brought up from town:
When the Democratic Keystone told the workers, "Vote for Hay",
  Then another blessed horse fell down!

When the polling day was over, and the promising was done—
  The promises that never would be kept
Then O'Sullivan came homeward at the sinking of the sun,
  To the Ministerial Bench he slowly crept.
When his colleagues said, "Who won it? Is our banner waving high?
  Has the Ministry retained Glen Innes Town?"
Then the great man hesitated, and responded with a sigh—
  "There's another blessed seat gone down!"

The Evening News, 27 October 1903

THE BALLAD OF THE CARPET BAG

The political season being now upon us, the following ballad may be appropriate

Ho! Darkies, don't you hear dose voters cryin',
  Pack dat carpet bag!
You must get to de Poll, you must get there flyin';
  Pack dat carpet bag!
You must travel by de road, you must travel by de train,
And the things what you've done you will have to explain,
And the things what you've promised, you must promise 'em again.
  Pack dat carpet bag!

Hear dem voters callin'!
  Pack de clean boiled rag.
For there's grass in the west, and the rain am fallin'.
  Pack dat carpet bag!
You must pack up a volume of Coghlan's Figures,
  Pack dat carpet bag!
And a lot o' little jokes to amuse those niggers.
  Pack dat carpet bag!
You must wheedle all de gals with a twinkle of your eye,
You must bob down your head when de eggs begin to fly.
Oh! those eggs what they're saving, and they'll throw 'em by and by.
  Pack dat carpet bag!

Hear dem voters callin'!
  Pack de clean boiled rag.
For there's grass in the west, and the rain am fallin'.
  Pack dat carpet bag!
You must get upon a stump, you must practise speakin',
  Pack dat carpet bag!
You must follow Georgie Reid or Alfred Deakin.
  Pack dat carpet bag!
You must come to de scratch, or you're bound to fail,
For it ain't any time to be sittin' on de rail,
Or de votes that you'll get—they won't keep you out o' jail.
  Pack dat carpet bag!

Hear dem voters callin'!
  Pack de clean boiled rag.
For there's grass in the west, and the rain am fallin',
  Pack dat carpet bag!

And supposin' that you're beat, and you feel like cryin',
 Pack dat carpet bag!
You must hustle back to work—just to keep from dyin'.
 Pack dat carpet bag!
You must travel second-class when you travel by de train,
For you haven't got a pass on de end of your chain,
While the other fellow's packing for de great campaign.
 Pack dat carpet bag!

Hear dem voters callin'!
 Pack de clean boiled rag.
For there's grass in the west, and the rain am fallin'.
 Pack dat carpet bag!

The Evening News, 21 November 1903

A NERVOUS GOVERNOR-GENERAL

We read in the press that Lord Northcote is here
 To take up Lord Tennyson's mission.
'Tis pleasant to find they have sent us a Peer,
 And a man of exalted position.
It's his business to see that the Radical horde
 From loyalty's path does not swerve us;
But his tastes, and the task, don't seem quite in accord
 For they say that His Lordship is nervous.

Does he think that wild animals walk in the street,
 Where the wary marsupial is hopping?
Does he think that the snake and the platypus meet
 And "bail up" the folk who go shopping?
And that boomerangs fly round the scared passer-by
 Who has come all this way to observe us.
While the blackfellow launches a spear at his eye?
 —No wonder His Lordship is nervous.

Does he think that with callers he'll be overtasked,
 From a baronet down to a barber?
Does he dream of the number of times he'll be asked
 "What he thinks of our Beautiful Harbour?"
Does he sadly reflect on the sorrows that ding
 Round his task? (From such sorrows preserve us!)
He must hear John See speak and O'Sullivan sing,
 —It's enough to make any man nervous.

Does he think he'll be waked in the dead of the night
 From Melbourne to go willy-nilly,
To live at the Federal Capital site
 At Tumut or Wagra-go-billy?
Well, the Melbournites may let the Capital go
 (Here we wink with one eye, please observe us!)
But not in a hurry! By no means! Oh, no!
 He has not the least need to be nervous!

The Evening News, 26 January 1904

THE FITZROY BLACKSMITH
With Apologies to Longfellow

Under the spreading deficit,
  The Fitzroy Smithy stands;
The smith, a spendthrift man is he,
  With too much on his hands;
But the muscles of his brawny jaw
  Are strong as iron bands.

Pay out, pay out, from morn till night,
  You can hear the sovereigns go;
Or you'll hear him singing "Old Folks at Home",
  In a deep bass voice and slow,
Like a bullfrog down in the village well
  When the evening sun is low.

The Australian going "home" for loans
  Looks in at the open door;
He loves to see the imported plant,
  And to hear the furnace roar,
And to watch the private firms smash up
  Like chaff on the threshing-floor.

Toiling, rejoicing, borrowing,
  Onward through life he goes;
Each morning sees some scheme begun
  That never sees its close.
Something unpaid for, someone done,
  Has earned a night's repose.

The Evening News, 13 February 1904

THE SEVEN AGES OF WISE
A Post-Shakespearian Fragment

Parliament's a stage,
And all the Politicians merely players!
They have their exits and their entrances,
And Wise doth in his time play many parts,
His acts being seven changes.

First the Runner,
With spiked shoe he spurns the cinder track,
And just for once runs straight.

The next the Student,
Burning the midnight oil with Adam Smith
For Cobden medals.

Next the youthful member,
With shining morning face, creeping between
Two seasoned leaders into place and power
Before his whiskers grow.

The next the bravo.
Jealous of greater men, he cries,
"Ha, Ha! Beware Bernardo's dagger!" —and would strike
His friend i' th' back.

Then comes a sudden change.
Once more a child, he comes with quick-turned coat,
New friends, new doctrines, and new principles,
Lets Friedman loose, and wrecks the Government.
Then leads the horny-handed sons of toil
By many a specious promise to their doom
In Arbitration Courts.

Last scene of all,
That ends this strange, disastrous history.
He aims at Judgeships and Commissionerships,
But, failing, passes on to mere oblivion.
Sans place, sans power, sans pay, sans everything.

The Evening News, 11 April 1904

THE RHYME OF THE O'SULLIVAN AND PRO BONO PUBLICO

Pro Bono Publico
 Went out the streets to scan,
And marching to and fro
 He met a seedy man,

Who did a tale unfold
 In solemn tones and slow,
And this is what he told
 Pro Bono Publico.

"For many years I led
 The people's onward march;
I was the 'Fountain Head',
 The 'Democratic Arch'.

"In more than regal state
 I used to sit and smile,
And bridges I'd donate,
 And railways by the mile.

"I pawned the country off
 For many million quid,
And spent it like a toff—
 So help me, Bob, I did.

"But now those times are gone,
 The wind blows cold and keen;
I sit and think upon
 The thing that I have been.

"And if a country town
 Its obligation shirks,
I press for money down
 To pay for water works.

"A million pounds or two
 Was naught at all to me—
And now I have to sue
 For paltry £ s d!

"Alas, that such a fate
 hould come to such a man,
Who once was called the Great —
 The great O'Sullivan!"

With weary steps and slow,
 With tears of sympathy
Pro Bono Publico
 Went sadly home to tea.

Remarking, as he went,
 With sad and mournful brow,
"The cash that party spent —
 I wish I had it now!"

The Evening News, 21 May 1904

"AVE CAESAR"

Long ago the Gladiators,
 When the call to combat came,
Marching past the massed spectators,
 Hailed the Emp'ror with acclaim!
Voices ringing with the fury
 Of the strife so soon to be,
Cried, "0 Caesar, morituri
 salutamus te!'

Nowadays the massed spectators
 See the unaccustomed sight—
Legislative gladiators
 Marching to their last great fight;
Young and old, obscure and famous,
 Hand to hand and knee to knee—
Hear the war-cry, "Salutamus
 morituri te!'

Fight! Nor be the fight suspended
 Till the corpses strew the plain.
Ere the grisly strife be ended
 Five and thirty must be slain.
Slay and spare not, lest another
 Haply may discomfit thee:
Brother now must war with brother
 "Salutamus te!'

War-worn vet'ran, skilled debater,
 Trickster famed of bridge and road,
Now for each grim gladiator
 Gapes Oblivion's drear abode.
Should the last great final jury
 Turn their thumbs down—it must be!
"Aye, Caesar, morituri
 salutamus te!'

The Evening News, 16 July 1904

THE PREMIER AND THE SOCIALIST

The Premier and the Socialist
 Were walking through the State:
They wept to see the Savings Bank
 Such funds accumulate.
"If these were only cleared away,"
 They said, "it would be great."

"If three financial amateurs
 Controlled them for a year,
Do you suppose," the Premier said,
 "That they would get them clear?"
"I think so," said the Socialist;
 "They would — or very near!"

"If we should try to raise some cash
 On assets of our own,
Do you suppose," the Premier said,
 "That we could float a loan?"
"I doubt it," said the Socialist,
 And groaned a doleful groan.

"Oh, Savings, come and walk with us!"
 The Premier did entreat;
"A little walk, a little talk,
 Away from Barrack Street;
My Socialistic friend will guide
 Your inexperienced feet."

"We do not think," the Savings said,
 "A Socialistic crank,
Although he chance just now to hold
 A legislative rank,
Can teach experienced Banking men
 The way to run a Bank."

The Premier and the Socialist
 They passed an Act or so
To take the little Savings out
 And let them have a blow.
"We'll teach the Banks," the Premier said,

"The way to run the show.

"There's Tom Waddell—in Bank Finance
 Can show them what is what.
I used to prove not long ago
 His Estimates were rot.
But that—like many other things—
 I've recently forgot.

"Advances on a dried-out farm
 Are what we chiefly need,
And loans to friends of Ms.L.A.
 Are very good, indeed,
See how the back-block Cockatoos
 Are rolling up to feed."

"But not on us," the Savings cried,
 Falling a little flat,
"We didn't think a man like you
 Would do a thing like that;
For most of us are very small,
 And none of us are fat."

"This haughty tone," the Premier said,
 "Is not the proper line;
Before I'd be dictated to
 My billet I'd resign!"
"How brightly," said the Socialist,
 "Those little sovereigns shine."

The Premier and the Socialist
 They had their bit of fun;
They tried to call the Savings back
 But answer came there none,
Because the back-block Cockatoos
 Had eaten every one.

The Evening News, 10 November 1904

THE BALLAD OF M. T. NUTT AND HIS DOG

The Honourable M. T. Nutt
 About the bush did jog,
Till, passing by a settler's hut,
 He stopped and bought a dog.

Then started homewards full of hope,
 Alas, that hopes should fail!
The dog pulled back and took the rope
 Beneath the horse's tail.

The Horse remarked, "I would be soft
 Such liberties to stand!"
"Oh dog," he said, "Go up aloft,
 Young man, go on the land!"

The Evening News, 17 December 1904

THE MAN FROM GOONDIWINDI, Q.

I

This is the sunburnt bushman who
Came down from Goondiwindi, Q.

II

This is the Push from Waterloo
That spotted the sunburnt bushman who
Came down from Goondiwindi, Q.

III

These are the wealthy uncles—two,
Part of the Push from Waterloo
That spotted the sunburnt bushman who
Came down from Goondiwindi, Q.

IV

This is the game, by no means new,
Played by the wealthy uncles—two,
Part of the Push from Waterloo
That spotted the sunburnt bushman who
Came down from Goondiwindi, Q.

V

This is the trooper dressed in blue
Who busted the game by no means new
Played by the wealthy uncles—two,
Part of the Push from Waterloo
That spotted the sunburnt bushman who
Came down from Goondiwindi, Q.

VI

This is the magistrate who knew
Not only the trooper dressed in blue,
But also the game by no means new,

And likewise the wealthy uncles—two,
And ditto the Push from Waterloo
That spotted the sunburnt bushman who
Came down from Goondiwindi, Q.

VII

This is the tale that has oft gone through
On western plains where the skies are blue,
Till the native bear and the kangaroo
Have heard of the magistrate who knew
Not only the trooper dressed in blue,
But also the game by no means new,
And likewise the wealthy uncles—two,
And ditto the Push from Waterloo
That spotted the sunburnt bushman who
Came down from Goondiwindi, Q.

The Evening News, 17 December 1904

THE DAM THAT KEELE BUILT
Being the History of the Cataract Dam in Verse

This is the dam that Keele built
This is the stream that brought the water to fill the dam that Keele built;

This is the Water and Sewer Brigade,
That measured the stream that brought the water to fill the dam that Keele built.

This is the Engineer by Trade—
Head of the Water and Sewer Brigade—
Who measured the stream that brought the water to fill the dam that Keele built.

These are the Calculations made
By the Eminent Engineer by Trade,
Head of the Water and Sewer Brigade,
Who measured the stream that brought the water to fill the dam that Keele built.

This is the Scornful Mr Wade,
Who sneered at the Calculations made
By the Eminent Engineer by Trade,
Head of the Water and Sewer Brigade,
Who measured the stream that brought the water to fill the dam that Keele built.

This is the Minister quite dismayed,
At the sight of the Scornful Mr Wade,
Who sneered at the Calculations made
By the Eminent Engineer by Trade,
Head of the Water and Sewer Brigade,
Who measured the stream that brought the water to fill the dam that Keele built.

This is the Sydneyite afraid,
That a serious blunder will be made,
Because of the Minister, quite dismayed,
At the sight of the Scornful Mr Wade,
Who sneered at the Calculations made
By the Eminent Engineer by Trade,
Head of the Water and Sewer Brigade,
Who measured the stream that brought the water to fill the dam that Keele built.

The Evening News, 27 February 1905

THE INCANTATION
Scene: Federal Political Arena

A darkened cave. In the middle a cauldron boiling.
Enter the three witches.

1ST WITCH: Thrice hath the Federal Jackass brayed. 2ND WITCH: Once the Bruce-Smith War-horse neighed.

3RD WITCH: So Georgie comes, 'tis time, 'tis time, Around the cauldron to chant our rhyme.

1ST WITCH: In the cauldron boil and bake
Fillet of a tariff snake,
Home-made flannels—mostly cotton,
Apples full of moths, and rotten,
Lamb that perished in the drought,
Starving stock from "furthest out",
Drops of sweat from cultivators,
Sweating to feed legislators. Grime from a white stoker's nob,
Toiling at a nigger's job.
Thus the great Australian Nation,
Seeks political salvation.

ALL: Double, double, toil and trouble, Fire burn, and cauldron bubble.

2ND WITCH: Heel-taps from the threepenny bars, Ash from Socialist cigars.
Leathern tongue of boozer curst
With the great Australian thirst,
Two-up gambler keeping dark,
Loafer sleeping in the park
Drop them in to prove the sequel,
All men are born free and equal.

ALL: Double, double, toil and trouble, Fire burn, and cauldron bubble.

3RD WITCH: Lung of Labour agitator,
Gall of Isaacs turning traitor;
Spleen that Kingston has revealed,
Sawdust stuffing out of Neild;

Mix them up, and then combine
With duplicity of Lyne,
Alfred Deakin's gift of gab,
Mix the gruel thick and slab.

ALL: Double, double! Boil and bubble!
Heav'n help Australia in her trouble.

HECATE: Oh, well done, I commend your pains,
And everyone shall share i' the gains,
And now about the cauldron sing,
Enchanting all that you put in.
Round about the cauldron go,
In the People's rights we'll throw,
Cool it with an Employer's blood,
Then the charm stands firm and good,
And thus with chaos in possession,
Ring in the coming Fed'ral Session.

The Evening News, 6 May 1905

A MOTOR COURTSHIP

Into her presence he gaily pranced,
A very fat spark, and a bit advanced.

With a Samson tread on the earth he trod,
He was stayed and gaitered, and fifty odd.

And she was a tulip just unfurled,
The sweetest thing in the motor world.

Her body was one of which poets dreamed;
Eighteen—twenty, or so she seemed.

Her air was haughty, her spirit proud,
But properly governed, as all allowed.

"Pity," he said, "my sad condition;
My heart's in a state of advanced ignition.

"Ask me to do some desperate deed,
And I'll do it at once at my topmost speed."

"Sir," said the maiden, "pray be seated;
I fear from your bearing you're somewhat heated.

"And I trust that a timely lubrication
Of throttle will cool your circulation."

As a well-made mixture she indicated,
With joy and gladness he radiated.

"Oh, come," said he, "in this soft spring weather,
Let us run over the world together!"

But she slipped his clutch with a gesture mocking,
"Your heart," she said; "I can hear it knocking.

"You haven't the gear at my pace to last;
Both men and motors—I like them fast.

"And I think that in me you have missed your mission;

You are only an old-style tube-ignition!"

With a sidelong motion he left the place;
For weal or woe he was off his base.

He drove his car to the cliffs of Dover,
Made one short circuit and ran her over.

And the stormy Petrol her rest is taking,
Where only the wild waves do the "brakeing".

The Evening News, 20 January 1906

WISDOM OF HAFIZ: THE PHILOSOPHER TAKES TO RACING

My son, if you go to the races to battle with Ikey and Mo,
Remember, it's seldom the pigeon can pick out the eye of the crow;
Remember, they live by the business; remember, my son, and go slow!

If ever an owner should tell you, "Back mine"—don't you be such a flat.
He knows his own cunning no doubt—does he know what the others are at?
Find out what he's frightened of most, and invest a few dollars on that.

Walk not in the track of the trainer, nor hang round the rails at his stall.
His wisdom belongs to his patron—shall he give it to one and to all?
When the stable is served he may tell you—and his words are like jewels let fall.

Run wide of the tipster, who whispers that Borak is sure to be first,
He tells the next mug that he meets with a tale with the placings reversed;
And, remember, of judges of racing, the jockey's the absolute worst.

When they lay three to one on the field, and the runners are twenty-and-two,
Take a pull at yourself; take a pull—it's a mighty big field to get through.
Is the club handicapper a fool? If a fool is about, perhaps it's you!

Beware of the critic who tells you the handicap's absolute rot,
For this is chucked in, and that's hopeless, and somebody ought to be shot.
How is it he can't make a fortune himself when he knows such a lot?

From tipsters, and jockeys, and trials, and gallops, the glory has gone,
For this is the wisdom of Hafiz that sages have pondered upon,
"The very best tip in the world is to see the commission go on!"

The Evening News, 21 April 1906

THE DAUNTLESS THREE
With Apologies to the Shade of Macaulay

Chris Watson, of the Parliament,
 By his Caucus Gods he swore
That the great Labor Party
 Should suffer wrong no more.
By his Caucus Gods he swore it,
 And named a trysting day,
And bade his Socialists ride forth,
 East and west and south and north,
 To summon his array.

East and west and south and north
 The Socialists ride fast,
And every town in New South Wales
 Has heard their trumpet's blast.
Shame to the false elector
 Who lingers in his hole,
While Watson and his myrmidons
 Are riding to the poll.

Then up spake brave Horatius Gould,
 And a Liberal proud was he,
"Now, who will stand on either hand
 And face the foe with me?"
Then out spake bold Herminius Millen,
 And Walker out spake he,
"We will abide on either side
 And win a seat with thee."

"'Tis well", quoth brave Horatius,
 "As thou sayest, so let it be."
And straight against the proletaire
 Forth went the dauntless three.
 (Issue impending)

The Evening News, 8 December 1906

OLD SCHOOLDAYS

Awake, of Muse, the echoes of a day
Long past, the ghosts of mem'ries manifold—
Youth's memories that once were green and gold
But now, alas, are grim and ashen grey.

The drowsy schoolboy wakened up from sleep,
First stays his system with substantial food,
Then off for school with tasks half understood,
Alas, alas, that cribs should be so cheap!

The journey down to town—'twere long to tell
The storm and riot of the rabble rout;
The wild Walpurgis revel in and out
That made the ferry boat a floating hell.

What time the captive locusts fairly roared:
And bulldog ants, made stingless with a knife,
Climbed up the seats and scared the very life
From timid folk, who near jumped overboard.

The hours of lessons—hours with feet of clay
Each hour a day, each day more like a week:
While hapless urchins heard with blanched cheek
The words of doom "Come in on Saturday".

The master gowned and spectacled, precise,
Trying to rule by methods firm and kind
But always just a little bit behind
The latest villainy, the last device,

Born of some smoothfaced urchin's fertile brain
To irritate the hapless pedagogue,
And first involve him in a mental fog
Then "have" him with the same old tale again.

The "bogus" fight that brought the sergeant down
To that dark corner by the old brick wall,
Where mimic combat and theatric brawl
Made noise enough to terrify the town.

But on wet days the fray was genuine,
When small boys pushed each other in the mud
And fought in silence till thin streams of blood
Their dirty faces would incarnadine.

The football match or practice in the park
With rampant hoodlums joining in the game
Till on one famous holiday there came
A gang that seized the football for a lark.

Then raged the combat without rest or pause,
Till one, a hero, Hawkins unafraid
Regained the ball, and later on displayed
His nose knocked sideways in his country's cause.

Before the mind quaint visions rise and fall,
Old jokes, old sports, old students dead and gone:
And some that lead us still, while some toil on
As rank and file, but "Grammar" children all.

And he, the pilot, who has laid the course
For all to steer by, honest, unafraid —
Truth is his beacon light, so he has made
The name of the old School a living force.

The Sydneian, August 1907

"WE'RE ALL AUSTRALIANS NOW"

Australia takes her pen in hand,
 To write a line to you,
To let you fellows understand,
 How proud we are of you.

From shearing shed and cattle run,
 From Broome to Hobson's Bay,
Each native-born Australian son,
 Stands straighter up

The man who used to "hump his drum",
 On far-out Queensland runs,
Is fighting side by side with some
 Tasmanian farmer's sons.

The fisher-boys dropped sail and oar
 To grimly stand the test,
Along that storm-swept Turkish shore,
 With miners from the west.

The old state jealousies of yore
 Are dead as Pharaoh's sow, We're not
State children any more
 We're all Australians now!

Our six-starred flag that used to fly,
 Half-shyly to the breeze,
Unknown where older nations ply
 Their trade on foreign seas,

Flies out to meet the morning blue
 With Vict'ry at the prow;
For that's the flag the Sydney flew,
 The wide seas know it now!

The mettle that a race can show,
 Is proved with shot and steel,
And now we know what nations know
 And feel what nations feel.

The honoured graves beneath the crest
 Of Gaba Tepe hill,
May hold our bravest and our best,
 But we have brave men still.

With all our petty quarrels done,
 Dissensions overthrown,
We have, through what you boys have done,
 A history of our own.

Our old world diff'rences are dead,
 Like weeds beneath the plough, For English,
Scotch, and Irish-bred,
 They're all Australians now!

So now we'll toast the Third Brigade,
 That led Australia's van,
For never shall their glory fade
 In minds Australian.

Fight on, fight on, unflinchingly,
 Till right and justice reign.
Fight on, fight on, till Victory
 Shall send you home again.

And with Australia's flag shall fly
A spray of wattle bough,
To symbolise our unity,
We're all Australians now.

Published as an open letter to the troops, 1915

AUSTRALIA TODAY 1916

They came from the lower levels
 Deep down in the Brilliant mine;
From the wastes where the whirlwind revels,
 Whirling the leaves of pine.

On the western plains, where the Darling flows,
 And the dust storms wheel and shift,
The teamster loosened his yokes and bows,
 And turned his team adrift.

On the western stations, far and wide,
 There's many an empty pen,
For the "ringers" have cast the machines aside
 And answered the call for men.

On the lucerne flats where the stream runs slow,
 And the Hunter finds the sea,
The women are driving the mowers now,
 With the children at their knee.

For the men have gone, as a man must go,
 At the call of the rolling drums;
For the men have sworn that the Turks shall know
 When the old battalion comes.

Column of companies by the right,
 Steady in strong array,
With the sun on the bayonets gleaming bright,
 The battalion marched away.

They battled, the old battalion,
 Through the toil of the training camps,
Sweated and strove at lectures,
 By the light of the stinking lamps.

Marching, shooting, and drilling;
 Steady and slow and stern;
Awkward and strange, but willing
 All of their job to learn.

Learning to use the rifle;
 Learning to use the spade;
Deeming fatigue a trifle
 During each long parade.

Till at last they welded
 Into a concrete whole,
And there grew in the old battalion
 A kind of battalion's soul.

Brotherhood never was like it;
 Friendship is not the word;
But deep in that body of marching men
 The soul of a nation stirred.

And like one man with a single thought
 Cheery and confident;
Ready for all that the future brought,
 The old battalion went.

Column of companies by the right,
 Steady in strong array,
With the sun on the bayonets gleaming bright,
 The battalion marched away.

How shall we tell of their landing
 By the hills where the foe were spread,
And the track of the old battalion
 Was marked by the Turkish dead?

With the dash that discipline teaches,
 Though the hail of the shrapnel flew,
And the forts were raking the beaches,
 And the toll of the dead men grew.

They fixed their grip on the gaunt hillside
 With a pluck that has won them fame;
And the home-folks know that the dead men died
 For the pride of Australia's name.

Column of companies by the right,
 To the beat of the rolling drums;
With honours gained in a stirring fight

Collected Poetry

The old Battalion comes!

Written 1916: date of publication unknown

THE ARMY MULES

Oh the airman's game is a showman's game for we all of us watch him go
With his roaring soaring aeroplane and his bombs for the blokes below,
Over the railways and over the dumps, over the Hun and the Turk,
You'll hear him mutter, "What ho, she bumps," when the Archies get to work.
But not of him is the song I sing, though he follow the eagle's flight,
And with shrapnel holes in his splintered wing comes home to his roost at night.
He may silver his wings on the shining stars, he may look from the throne on high,
He may follow the flight of the wheeling kite in the blue Egyptian sky,
But he's only a hero built to plan, turned out by the Army schools,
And I sing of the rankless, thankless man who hustles the Army mules.

Now where he comes from and where he lives is a mystery dark and dim,
And it's rarely indeed that the General gives a D.S.O. to him.
The stolid infantry digs its way like a mole in a ruined wall;
The cavalry lends a tone, they say, to what were else but a brawl;
The Brigadier of the Mounted Fut like a cavalry Colonel swanks
When he goeth abroad like a gilded nut to receive the General's thanks;
The Ordnance man is a son of a gun and his lists are a standing joke;
You order, "Choke arti Jerusalem one" for Jerusalem artichoke.
The Medicals shine with a number nine, and the men of the great R.E.,
Their Colonels are Methodist, married or mad, and some of them all the three;
In all these units the road to fame is taught in the Army schools,
But a man has got to be born to the game when he tackles the Army mules.

For if you go where the depots are as the dawn is breaking grey,
By the waning light of the morning star as the dust cloud clears away,
You'll see a vision among the dust like a man and a mule combined—
It's the kind of thing you must take on trust for its outlines aren't defined,
A thing that whirls like a spinning top and props like a three legged stool,
And you find its a long-legged Queensland boy convincing an Army mule.
And the rider sticks to the hybrid's hide like paper sticks to a wall,
For a "magnoon" Waler is next to ride with every chance of a fall,
It's a rough-house game and a thankless game, and it isn't a game for a fool,
For an army's fate and a nation's fame may turn on an army mule.

And if you go to the front-line camp where the sleepless outposts lie,
At the dead of night you can hear the tramp of the mule train toiling by.
The rattle and clink of a leading-chain, the creak of the lurching load,

As the patient, plodding creatures strain at their task in the shell-torn road,
Through the dark and the dust you may watch them go till the dawn is grey in the sky,
And only the watchful pickets know when the "All-night Corps" goes by.
And far away as the silence falls when the last of the train has gone,
A weary voice through the darkness: "Get on there, men, get on!"
It isn't a hero, built to plan, turned out by the modern schools,
It's only the Army Service man a-driving his Army mules.

The Kia-Ora Coo-ee, March 1918

SWINGING THE LEAD

Said the soldier to the Surgeon, "I've got noises in me head
And a kind o' filled up feeling after every time I'm fed;
I can sleep all night on picket, but I can't sleep in my bed".
 And the Surgeon said,
 "That's Lead!"

Said the soldier to the surgeon, "Do you think they'll send me back?
For I really ain't adapted to be carrying a pack
Though I've humped a case of whisky half a mile upon my back".
 And the Surgeon said,
 "That's Lead!"

"And my legs have swelled up cruel, I can hardly walk at all,
But when the Taubes come over you should see me start to crawl;
When we're sprinting for the dugout, I can easy beat 'em all".
 And the Surgeon said,
 "That's Lead."

So they sent him to the trenches where he landed safe and sound,
And fie drew his ammunition, just about two fifty round:
"Oh, Sergeant, what's this heavy stuff I've got to hump around?"
 And the Sergeant said,
 "That's Lead!"

The Kia-ora Coo-ee, April 1918

MOVING ON

In this war we're always moving,
  Moving on;
When we make a friend another friend has gone;
Should a woman's kindly face
Make us welcome for a space,
Then it's boot and saddle, boys, we're
  Moving on.

In the hospitals they're moving,
  Moving on;
They're here today, tomorrow they are gone;
When the bravest and the best
Of the boys you know "go west",
Then you're choking down your tears and
  Moving on.

The Kia-ora Coo-ee, May 1918

HAWKER THE STANDARD BEARER

The grey gull sat on a floating whale,
  On a floating whale sat he,
And he told his tale of the storm and the gale,
And the ships that he saw with steam and sail,
  As he flew by the Northern Sea.

"I have seen a sign that is strange and new,
  That I never before did see:
A flying ship that roared as it flew,
The storm and the tempest driving through,
It carried a flag and it carried a crew,
  Now what would that be?" said he.

"And the flag was a Jack with stars displayed,
  A flag that is new to me;
For it does not ply in the Northern trade,
But it drove through the storm-wrack unafraid,
  Now, what is that flag?" said he.

"I have seen that flag that is starred with white,"
  Said a southern gull, said he,
"And I saw it fly in a bloody fight,
When the raider Emden turned in flight,
  And crashed on the Cocos lee."

"And who are these folk whose flag is first
  Of all the flags that fly
To dare the storm and the fog accurst,
Of the great North Sea where the bergs are nursed,
  And the Northern Lights ride high?"

"The Australian folk," said a lone sea-mew,
  "The Australian flag," said he.
"It is strange that a folk that is far and few
Should fly their flag where there never flew
  Another flag!" said he.

"I have followed their flag in the fields of France,
  With its white stars flying free,
And no misfortune and no mischance

Could turn them back from their line of advance,
 Or the line that they held," said he.

"Wherever there's ever a rule to break,
 Wherever they oughtn't to be,
With a death to dare and a risk to take,
A track to find or a way to make,
 You will find them there," said he.

"They come from a land that is parched with thirst,
 An inland land," said he,
"On risk and danger their breed is nursed,
And thus it happens their flag is first
 To fly in the Northern Sea."

"Though Hawker perished, he overcame
 The risks of the storm and the sea,
And his name shall be written in stars of flame,
On the topmost walls of the Temple of Fame,
 For the rest of the world to see."

Smith's Weekly, 24 May 1919

CASSIDY'S EPITAPH

Here lies a bloke who's just gone West,
  A Number One Australian;
He took his gun and did his best
  To mitigate the alien.
So long as he could get to work
  He needed no sagacity;
A German, Austrian, or Turk,
  Were all the same to Cassidy.

Whenever he could raise "the stuff" —
  A liquor deleterious
The question when he'd have enough
  Was apt to be mysterious.
'Twould worry prudent folks a lot
  Through mental incapacity;
If he could keep it down or not,
  Was all the same to Cassidy.

And when the boys would start a dance,
  In honour of Terpsichore,
'Twas just an even-money chance
  You'd find him rather shickery.
But once he struck his proper stride,
  And heard the band's vivacity,
The jazz, the tango, or the slide
  Was all the same to Cassidy.

And now he's gone to face the Light,
  With all it may reveal to him,
A life without a drink or fight
  Perhaps may not appeal to him;
But when St Peter calls the roll
  Of men of proved tenacity,
You'll find the front-rank right-hand man
  Will answer: "Here...Cassidy."

Smith's Weekly, 14 June 1919

BOOTS

"The Australian boots were the best of any issued to the Allied forces."

We've travelled per Joe Gardiner, a humping of our swag
 In the country of the Gidgee and Belar.
We've swum the Di'mantina with our raiment in a bag,
 And we've travelled per superior motor car,
But when we went to Germany we hadn't any choice,
 No matter what our training or pursuits,
For they gave us no selection 'twixt a Ford or Rolls de Royce
 So we did it in our good Australian boots.

They called us "mad Australians"; they couldn't understand
 How officers and men could fraternise,
They said that we were "reckless", we were "wild, and out of hand",
 With nothing great or sacred to our eyes.
But on one thing you could gamble, in the thickest of the fray,
 Though they called us volunteers and raw recruits,
You could track us past the shell holes, and the tracks were all one way
 Of the good Australian ammunition boots.

The Highlanders were next of kin, the Irish were a treat,
 The Yankees knew it all and had to learn,
The Frenchmen kept it going, both in vict'ry and defeat,
 Fighting grimly till the tide was on the turn.
And our army kept beside 'em, did its bit and took its chance,
 And I hailed our newborn nation and its fruits,
As I listened to the clatter on the cobblestones of France
 Of the good Australian military boots.

Smith's Weekly, 5 July 1919

THE OLD TIN HAT

In the good old days when the Army's ways were simple and unrefined,
With a stock to keep up their chins in front, and a pigtail down behind,
When the only light in the barracks at night was a candle of grease or fat,
When they put the extinguisher on the light, they called it the Old Tin Hat.

Now, a very great man is the C. in C., for he is the whole of the show—
The reins and the whip and the driver's hand that maketh the team to go—
But the road he goes is a lonely road, with ever a choice to make,
When he comes to a place where the roads divide, which one is the road to take.
For there's one road right, and there's one road wrong, uphill, or over the flat,
And one road leads to the Temple of Fame, and one to the Old Tin Hat.

And a very great man is the man who holds an Army Corps command,
For he hurries his regiments here and there as the C. in C. has planned.
By day he travels about in state and stirreth them up to rights,
He toileth early and toileth late, and sitteth up half the nights;
But the evening comes when the candle throws twin shadows upon the mat,
And one of the shadows is like a wreath, and one like an Old Tin Hat.

And a very proud man is the Brigadier at the sound of the stately tread
Of his big battalions marching on, as he rides with his staff ahead.
There's never a band to play them out, and the bugle's note is still,
But he hears two tunes in the gentle breeze that blows from over the hill.
And one is a tune in a stirring key, and the other is faint and flat,
For one is the tune of "My new C.B." and the other, "My Old Tin Hat."

And the Colonel heading his regiment is life and soul of the show,
It's "Column of route", "Form troops", "Extend", and into the fight they go;
He does not duck when the air is full of the "wail of the whimpering lead",
He does not scout for the deep dugout when the 'planes are overhead;
He fears not hog, nor devil, nor dog, and he'd scrap with a mountain cat,
But he goeth in fear of the Brigadier, and in fear of the Old Tin Hat.

Smith's Weekly, 12 July 1919

THE QUEST ETERNAL

O west of all that a man holds dear, on the edge of the Kingdom Come,
Where carriage is far too high for beer, and the pubs keep only rum,
On the sunburnt ways of the Outer Back, on the plains of the darkening scrub,
I have followed the wandering teamster's track, and it always led to a pub.

There's always in man some gift to show, some power he can command,
And mine is the Gift that I always know when a pub is close at hand;
I can pick them out on the London streets, though most of their pubs are queer,
Such solid-looking and swell retreats, with never a sign of beer.

In the march of the boys through Palestine when the noontide fervour glowed,
Over the desert in thirsty line our sunburnt squadrons rode.
They looked at the desert lone and drear, stone ridges and stunted scrub,
And said, "We should have had Ginger here, I bet he'd have found a pub!"

We started out in the noonday heat on a trip that was fast and far,
We took in one each side of the street to balance the blooming car,
But then we started a long dry run on a road we did not know,
In the blinding gleam of the noonday sun, with the dust as white as snow.

For twenty minutes without a drink we strove with our dreadful thirst,
But the chauffeur pointed and said, "I think — —," I answered "I saw it first!"
A pub with a good old-fashioned air, with bottles behind the blind,
And a golden tint in the barmaid's hair—I could see it all—in my mind

Ere ever the motor ceased its roar, ere ever the chauffeur knew,
I made a dash for the open door and madly darted through.
I looked for the barmaid, golden-crowned as they were in the good old time,
And—shades of Hennessy!—what I found was a wowser selling "lime!"
And the scoundrel said as he stopped to put on his lime-washed boots a rub,
"The Local Option voted it shut, it ain't no longer a pub!"

'Twas then I rose to my greatest heights in dignified retreat
(The greatest men in the world's great fights are those who are great in defeat).
I shall think with pride till the day I die of my confidence sublime,
For I looked the wowser straight in the eye, and asked for a pint of lime.

Smith's Weekly, 9 August 1919

THAT HALF-CROWN SWEEP
A Tale of the Territory

The run of Billabong-go-dry
 Is just beyond Lime Burner's Gap;
Its waterhole and tank supply
 Is excellent—upon the map.
But, lacking nature's liquid drench,
 The station staff are wont to try
With "Bob-in Sweeps" their thirst to quench,
 Or nearly quench, at Bong-go-dry.

The parson made five-yearly rounds
 That soil of arid souls to delve,
He wrote, "I'll come for seven pounds,
 Or I could stop away for twelve."
But lack of lucre brought about
 The pusillanimous reply:
"Our luxuries are all cut out,
 You'll have to come to Bong-go-dry."

Now rabbit skins were very high
 There'd been a kind of rabbit rush—
And what with traps and sticks they'd shy,
 The station blacks were very flush,
And each was taught his churchman's job,
 "When that one parson's plate comes roun'
No good you put in sprat or bob,
 Too quick you put in harp-a-crown."

The parson's word was duly kept,
 He came and did his bit of speak;
The boss remarked he hadn't slept
 So sound and well for many a week.
But Gilgai Jack and Monkey Jaw
 Regarded preaching as a crime
Against good taste; they said, "What for
 That one chap yabber all the time?"

Proceedings ceased: the boss's hat
 Was raked from underneath his chair;
The coloured congregation sat

And waited with expectant air.
At last from one far-distant seat
Where Gilgai's Mary'd been asleep,
There came a kind of plaintive bleat,
"Say, boss! Who won the harp-crown sweep?"

The Sydney Sportsman, 11 January 1922

Lightning Source UK Ltd.
Milton Keynes UK
UKHW010629090821
388558UK00001B/140